Ghostly Defenses

By

Joni Mayhan

Ghostly Defenses. Copyright 2014 by Joni Mayhan. All rights reserved. No part of this book may be used or reproduced in any manner without written permission from the author.

Cover photograph and design by Joni Mayhan.

Also by Joni Mayhan:

True Paranormal Non-fiction

Paranormal Fiction

Acknowledgments

This started off being a short guide but quickly took on a life of its own. I want to thank the people who have helped me over the years. Without them, I probably wouldn't be writing this book.

Barbara Williams is a gifted psychic medium who has been mentoring me for years. She taught me many of the practices I share in this book. I am eternally grateful for everything she's done for me.

Thanks also to Michael Cram, who has helped me on many occasions and has freely shared his wealth of knowledge with me. Through him, I learned about the practice of exorcism and the importance of keeping the faith. Thank you, Mike for always being there for me.

I am also thankful to my paranormal sidekick Sandy MacLeod who has progressed through this strange path alongside me, helping me every step of the way.

Thank you to Barb Wright for providing me with great editing and friendship. And to my paranormal investigating friends, Tina Aube, Marion Luoma, Steven Flaherty and Nancy Cram. Thank you, Alex Zaccheo for being my beta reader. To Kaden Mattison for teaching me how to manipulate my energy early on, and to George Brun for sharing his photos.

Thank you to my children, Laura and Trevor Mayhan, for putting up with having a strange mother, but loving me all the same. Also, thanks to my family who stuck by me while opening their minds to something strange and new.

And to the sensitives. You are not alone. There are many of us out there, as well.

This book is dedicated to my mentor Barbara Williams. Thank you for your knowledge, your guidance, and most of all, your friendship.

Table of Contents

Life as a Sensitive 1
Types of Hauntings 3
What is a Sensitive? 5
Clairaudience (clear hearing) 5
Clairsentience (clear feeling) 5
Clairtangience (clear touching) 6
Claircognizance (clear knowing) 7
Clairgustance (clear tasting) and Clairalience (clear smelling) 8
Clairvoyance (clear vision) 8
Empathy 8
    Grounding 10
    Shielding 10
    Tips for Unlocking Your Sixth Sense 11
Believe Your Abilities 11
Meditate 11
Pay Attention 12
Open Yourself Up 12
Believe in Yourself 15

Find Validation 17
Spirit Guides and Guardians 18
Document Everything 18
Research 18
Share Your Experiences 19
Everyone is Different 19

Using Pets for Validation 19
Practice Makes Perfect 21

Be Prepared 22
Protection from Others 25
Protecting Yourself during a Paranormal Investigation 27
Provoking 27
Respecting Their Space 28
Before the Investigation 29
State of Mind 29
Prayer 30
Medallions or Religious Symbols 31
Protection Stones 31
Cleansing and Charging Protective Stones 33
Protection Spray 34
Sage 34
Sea Salt 35
Grounding 35
Shielding 35
Spirit Guides and Guardians 35
Psychic Mediums 36
During the Investigation 37
After the Investigation 39
Paranormal Hangovers 40
What to Do if Something Follows You 45

(Above) The author investigating at the Houghton Mansion

Life as a Sensitive

I was born with a gift that scared me. I knew when ghosts were nearby.

It started when I was six years old. After my mother tucked me in, I would lie in my bed and look around my room, watching the shadows dance. At first it didn't scare me because I didn't know what I was looking at. It was just something I had always seen. It was normal.

Then I began hearing a ringing sound that accompanied the moving shadows. The sound swooped in, as if carried on the wind. It swirled around the room, coming closer and closer, until it zoomed away again. I wouldn't understand what it was until I was seven.

That was when I saw my first ghost.

It approached my bed, not stopping until it was mere inches away from me. I was so scared, I couldn't scream. All I could do was stare up at it in terror as the anger radiated from it like something I could see and touch. After a few minutes, I found my voice and screamed for my mother. It disappeared as she ran down the hallway.

When I told my parents about what I was seeing and experiencing, they told me it was just my imagination. "There is no such thing as ghosts," they said.

I have experiences ghostly activity throughout my life, never fully trusting what I was sensing was true. Was I really feeling ghosts? I didn't tell anyone for fear they'd think I was crazy. I kept the information to myself until I met some like-minded people, people who were sensitives like me.

I happened upon them in the usual way. I was drawn to the field that had held me captive for forty years. I joined a ghost hunting group. Through them, I met friends who were also able to sense and feel ghosts, and I began to learn more about my abilities.

One thing I didn't count on, though, was the fact that nothing would ever remain the same. Once I tuned in to my ability, it grew and developed, much like a well-exercised muscle.

Opening that doorway changed everything in my life. I no longer suspected that ghosts and spirits were nearby; I knew it as clearly as I knew the sky was blue. The more I trusted my gift, the better it became. Something strange happened to me at that point, something I never could have anticipated. I became haunted and hunted by the very ghosts I was sensing.

They came out of nowhere. Ghosts began following me home from restaurants, stores, and even from the homes of friends. I had to get a hold of this gift before it got a hold of me. Unfortunately, before that could happen, I walked into a very bad situation I wasn't prepared for.

I picked up a malevolent attachment.

I was like a lamb, leading myself into a den filled with lions. I didn't understand the impact my ability had on the spirit world and how vulnerable it made me toward the darker energies.

I wrote this guide to help those who are like me. When I first started out I had no idea where to turn to. You can consider this your starting place to help you get to where you want to be.

Sometimes we all need a little push in the right direction.

Types of Hauntings	
Intelligent	The ghosts are aware of you, and can often interact with you. Personalities will differ, just as in life.
Residual	In a residual haunting, the atmosphere has absorbed the energy from an event. The haunting repeats itself consistently, like a movie clip playing over and over. The appearance of ghostly Civil War soldiers on the Gettysburg battlefield is one example of a residual haunting.
Poltergeist	A poltergeist can manipulate the physical environment. Items are frequently moved or thrown. It can injure the living. Poltergeist phenomena are not necessarily a haunting. They are often caused by a living person, typically an adolescent, who unknowingly releases high levels of energy.
Demonic	Demonic entities mock the Holy Trinity by repeating activities in threes. Scratches, foul odors, changes in the personalities of the people involved and heightened activity are characteristic of demonic activity.

(Above) A photo of spirit energy attempting to manifest. The investigator confirmed that no one was smoking, and it wasn't due to warm breath on a cold night.

Photo courtesy of George Brun

What is a Sensitive?

A sensitive is someone who senses ghosts or spirits. Typically, most sensitives only get a small piece of the puzzle, unlike true psychic mediums who get clearer, better-rounded messages. Many people believe that we are all born sensitive, but lose the ability as we leave childhood. Others feel that we can develop and sharpen our sensitive abilities. Here are several of the most common sensitive abilities:

Clairaudience (clear hearing)

This was the first ability to unfold for me. A person with clairaudient ability hears sounds or voices that others do not hear. For me, this came as a tone, similar to ear ringing. As it developed, I began to learn more about the ghosts or spirits based on the sound I was hearing.

Others with this ability hear actual voices in their mind, something I also get from time to time. It is easy to dismiss this voice as your own internal monologue, but with practice, it becomes easier to differentiate between the two.

The Difference Between Ghosts and Spirits	
Ghosts	**Spirits**
Ghosts are earthbound human souls who have chosen not to cross over into the light. This is often associated with sudden, traumatic deaths or those with unfinished business.	Spirits are souls who have crossed over into the light. They are often our relatives coming back to visit us, or guides and guardians who are here to help us.

Clairsentience (clear feeling)

Someone who is clairsentient feels ghost and spirit energy. Sometimes it is a physical sensation, like having the hairs on the back of your neck prickle.

I began developing this ability shortly after honing my clairaudient skills. When a ghost swoops in, it feels like someone has walked quietly into a room and is standing directly behind me.

Others with this ability sometimes feel nauseated when spirit or ghostly energy is present. One of my clairsentient friends feels a tingling on her scalp. She has learned to separate ghost from spirit by asking her spirit visitors to make the right side of her head tingle, since ghost energy has always affected her left side.

Another one of my friends feels a tightening in her chest when a ghost is nearby. I sometimes get an inner trembling inside my torso that accompanies the ear ringing. This is usually different for everyone. This is the way your body alerts you.

Clairtangience (clear touching)

Have you ever touched a haunted item and immediately started getting impressions of the person who last owned it? If so, then you might be clairtangient. This ability can also be applied to living people. A handshake can unleash a plethora of information to the clairtangient sensitive. Also called psychometry, this talent is not confined to small objects or people. Because everything contains energy, even touching a building or a wall can provide a sensitive with information.

My friend and I play a game we call "Find the Haunted Item." We go to antique stores and walk around the store separately until we find an item with a ghost attached to it. Then we send the other person into the general area to see if she can find it as well.

Being clairaudient, it is actually easy for me. I just follow the sound of the tone. As I come into the room, I can hear it very faintly. I'll play a game of warmer/colder until the sound grows louder and I'm standing directly in front of the object. Then I put my hand on it to feel for vibrations. Sometimes an image will pop into my head and I get an impression of the person who once owned the item.

"It's this lamp," I told my friend and she nodded. She felt it too.

This game helps us hone our sensitivities and prevents us from bringing home haunted items.

Claircognizance (clear knowing)

This ability is the little voice inside your head that tells you what to do. In some ways, it's similar to clairaudience with the exception that you just *know* information you shouldn't be able to know. It could come to you in a message or a thought.

You might meet someone for the first time and know personal information about him or her that comes to you in an instant. I was at the doctor's office for a routine check-up, when I decided to test this ability.

The nurse came into the room to take my blood pressure. As she was taking my vitals, I kept getting very clear images of her basking in the sun on a resort island with friends and family. I narrowed my eyes, wondering where that was coming from, and then the vision expanded. I saw her with a group of people who were family members, but not immediate family. I somehow knew she was single and didn't have any children. The people she went with might have been siblings. I had been getting impressions like this all my life, but I never had the courage to confirm them, so I took a deep breath and asked her about a necklace she had on. It was a gold seashell on a chain.

"Oh, yes. I got this when I was on vacation last week. I went to the Bahamas with my sister and her family. It was so nice there," she told me, then frowned as my blood pressure skyrocketed.

I walked out alternating between smiling and shaking my head.

Clairgustance (clear tasting) and Clairalience (clear smelling)

Typically, people with these abilities can walk through a haunted location and notice residual energy, identifying a smell or taste that was once prevalent in the area. One of my friends visited an old haunted asylum. When she got to the bakery, she began smelling the distinct smell of baking bread. Another time, the same friend smelled perfume in a dormitory room that once belonged to a woman who favored lilac scents.

Clairvoyance (clear vision)

A true clairvoyant has knowledge that can't be perceived by using the normal human senses. Clairvoyance often touches on most of the other *clair* abilities. People with this ability are often able to foresee future events or locate hidden information. Law enforcement agents often use clairvoyants to help find missing people. Clairvoyants garner their information through a variety of means. Like any of the other *clairs*, no two clairvoyants are alike. They just know things that other people don't.

They also have an uncanny ability to break through the invisible barrier to glean information about ghosts and spirits. Some clairvoyants can tell you what a ghost looks like and what they want, while others will be able to get more detailed information, such as names and family history.

Empathy

An empath is someone who feels what others are feeling. They are highly tuned in to the energy around them, especially with loved ones. If a close family member grows ill, the empath may feel the illness, too. Being around negative energy is also difficult for them.

Empaths are usually great with children and animals. They are also in touch with ghosts and spirits, reading their energy, as well.

Empaths often have a difficult time being in crowded places. The combined energy from masses of people makes it nearly unbearable for the empath to tolerate.

Empaths are also very good listeners. People often seek them out for advice because they always provide a shoulder to cry on. If empaths don't learn proper grounding and shielding practices, they often feel overwhelmed by their abilities.

(Above) A photo of Joni at the Houghton Mansion with an apparition.
Photo courtesy of Sue Cousineau

Grounding

Grounding is the practice of ridding your body of excess energy. This is effective for most sensitives. I use it frequently during the day to help me remain calm and focused. One method for doing this is as follows:

1. Imagine a white light above you.
2. With every breath, pull the white light into you, through the top of your head.
3. As you exhale, imagine the white light pushing negative energy down through your feet and into the ground.

Trees can be helpful for grounding, as well. Many sensitives ground themselves by hugging trees and imagining the negative energy sinking into the ground beneath them.

Shielding

Shielding is the practice of creating a bubble of protective energy around you to safeguard you from negative energy or ghost attachment. While there are many ways to do this, I found the following method to be effective.

1. Imagine an energy ball forming at your solar plexus, your upper abdomen near the diaphragm.
2. Pull it up and around you like a bubble and fill it with white light. I do this every day, asking for it to protect me for 24 hours. My mentor says that if you don't time it, the shield will only last for several hours.

Experienced energy workers can often expand their shield to cover the entire house or location.

A psychic medium or a talented energy worker can help you practice and develop this. This isn't something you can fully learn from a book. You should have guidance while developing this ability.

Tips for Unlocking Your Sixth Sense

Abilities come in all shapes and sizes. Some people have the ability to sense or communicate with ghosts. Others get visions of future events before they transpire. Some people have a mysterious ability to read other people, knowing what they are thinking or feeling without prior knowledge. Some abilities are more subtle. One of my friends is a very dedicated pet sitter. She often senses something is wrong with a dog before the owner does. This could be a useful tool in her field, providing that the pet owners buy into what she is telling them.

Believe Your Abilities

My mother didn't think she had a sixth sense until I pointed it out to her. I would often pick up the phone to call her, only to find her on the other end as she attempted to call me at the same time. She also has an uncanny ability to find front row parking spots. Sometimes having a sixth sense isn't as astounding as being able to predict the sex of someone's unborn baby. It might be as simple as trusting your intuition and not trying to push it away. It is a special gift that was given to you at birth. Embrace it and learn to use it.

Meditate

Spend a few minutes a day going deep into your mind and allow the rest of the world to fade away. You can do this all by yourself with a little instruction, or you can use one of the many self-guided meditation videos online. Mediation allows you to hone your thoughts down to their roots, discovering a place in your mind where the clatter and bustle of everyday life can't reach.

Pay Attention

Watch other people's reactions to what you say and do. Understand how body language and eye contact play a key role in how we interpret other people's feelings. Tune into what they tell you. Crossed arms may mean they're closing themselves off from the conversation. An inability to maintain eye contact could mean they aren't comfortable. Watch for non-verbal cues to see if they match what you're sensing. Because people with empathic abilities often sense what other people are feeling, sometimes even physically, they have the capability of understanding the moods and thought processes of others. Learning how to live with this ability could be a blessing. If someone is angry with you, it gives you a chance to unravel the anger before it becomes an issue.

Open Yourself Up

You should understand this door is difficult to close once you've opened it. Opening yourself up allows your abilities to flourish, but it also makes you vulnerable to ghostly attachments. This happened to me when I first explored my abilities. I learned how to open quickly, but I didn't understand the importance of learning to close it, too.

To open yourself, you need to understand the chakras of your body. Each serves a purpose in your overall health and wellbeing. There are seven chakras in the human body. Considered energy centers, they help you move energy through your body, keeping you physically and spiritually fit.

Chakra/Position	Function
Root – Base of spine	Survival – Money, food, shelter
Sacral – Lower abdomen	Wellbeing - Pleasure, sexuality
Solar Plexus – Upper abdomen	Confidence
Heart - Center of chest	Love and happiness
Throat – Throat	Communication
Third Eye – Forehead	Intuition and wisdom
Crown – Top of head	Spiritual connection

While all of the chakras are important for maintaining health and balance, the sixth and seventh chakras are responsible for the majority of your psychic impressions.

The Crown Chakra

The top of your head, or crown chakra is your connection to spiritual awakening. Many intuitives picture it as a lotus flower blooming. As you open it, you invite spiritual information to come to you.

Practice the visualization of opening and closing this chakra. Instead of a lotus flower, I visualize a door on the top of my head lifting open, allowing the wisdom of the universe to come inside. When I don't want to be open, I mentally close it and then lock it tightly with an imagined padlock.

Meditation can help you get better control of this. As you grow more comfortable exploring the recesses of your mind, it becomes easier to open and close this chakra at will. I found that working with a psychic medium helped me determine whether I was truly opening or not.

A lot of what we do as sensitives is something we have to figure out on our own. I think of it as driving a car with no steering wheel or brakes. Before I take it for a drive down the highway, I want to know how to control it better. Practice this at home first before you attempt to use it during an investigation.

I open myself when I want to communicate with the spirit world, but I remain closed the rest of the time. I see it as a beacon, welcoming the spirit world to share information with me. If I walked around with my crown chakra open all the time, it would make me more vulnerable for attachment or unwanted attention. I would probably be leading a parade of ghosts around me, which I assure you isn't something I want.

A talented psychic medium can help you learn more about keeping your chakras flowing freely. Ask for more information at your local metaphysical store. Many will offer classes as well.

The Third Eye Chakra

Many New Age researchers believe that the Third Eye Chakra is connected to the pineal gland, a rice-sized endocrine glance located in the center of the brain. This gland is responsible for producing melatonin, a hormone that helps regulate our sleep patterns. In animals, this gland plays a major role in hibernation, sexual development and breeding, as well as metabolism.

Unfortunately, as the brain ages, it begins to calcify as it collects mineral deposits such as calcium, fluoride, and phosphorous. This causes the pineal gland to become unreliable, resulting in lack of sleep, as well as closing you down psychically. Research has also shown that patients with Alzheimer's disease have pineal glands with a higher rate of calcification.

French philosopher Rene Descartes felt that the pineal gland was the seat of the soul, where mind and body meet.

Tips for keeping your pineal gland from calcifying:

- Avoid fluoride. Drink filtered water and use fluoride-free toothpaste. Some bottled water contains fluoride as well, so check the ingredients.
- Stay away from processed foods. Eat as many organic foods as possible. Processed meats can also contain fluoride.
- Restrict calcium supplements, but make sure to check with your physician first.
- Avoid sodas and sweets with refined sugars. Junk food also falls into this category.
- If you drink tea, ensure it's made from young leaves like in green tea.

Believe in Yourself

It takes a great deal of courage to admit you're a sensitive. Although many people accept the concept of the paranormal now more than ever, not everyone will understand or appreciate your abilities.

It took me years to get to the point where I talked about it freely. I worried that people would think I was crazy, and then alienate me. What I learned was twofold. Not everyone is going to believe you, but it doesn't make it untrue. You are what you are, despite how others feel about you. By opening up about my abilities, I actually gained more than I lost. Other people began admitting that they too had abilities. I've learned to trust what I'm feeling and not worry about what other people think about it. I share it when I feel it's appropriate and keep it to myself when it's not. Trust your judgment. It's probably not something you want to discuss at a job interview, but something you may share with friends.

Being intuitive can mean something different for each person. It's not a cookie cutter ability that you can outline and detail. It's something you will need to explore for yourself. Do you sometimes get a strong feeling about something for no apparent reason? Have you ever woken up with a strange premonition? Pay attention to the outcome. If you find some truth behind the impression, you will learn to trust it more.

Many people believe that we're all born with a sixth sense, but leave it undeveloped. Perhaps it's because many of us are told as children that we have an active imagination. It doesn't mean the abilities have disappeared. It just means that we need to dig a little deeper to find them and nurture them back to a useable level.

Others feel that psychic abilities are passed down through families. Sometimes the gift is hard to distinguish, as was the case with my mother. It's more than likely she was born with similar abilities as mine but she didn't pursue them and allow them to develop.

Find Validation

If you have a strong sense that something has happened to someone, follow through to see if it's accurate. I would often get impressions about people, but I never had the courage to ask them for validation. One day I simply took a deep breath and asked, only to find out that my intuition was right. It gave me the faith to keep trying.

This is also important because we sometimes misinterpret the clues. As an empath, I often pick up on people's moods. One time my friend was in a bad mood. My first impression was that it had to do with a recent event we attended, and that she was angry with me for something I said. Instead of allowing this thought to fester inside me, I asked her about it and discovered I was partially right. She was upset about the event, but not because of anything I said or did. Always ask if you can. It helps more than you can imagine.

I wanted to add a word of caution here, though, about bad news. Not everyone is eager to receive a psychic reading, especially if the news is bad. As you seek validation, always weigh the ramifications and make your decision based on whether the news will be welcomed and helpful.

For example, I had a dream that an acquaintance was brutally murdered. I've never had prophetic dreams before, so chances are it was just a dream. If I had told this poor woman, I would probably have caused her unnecessary stress over nothing. Months passed with no harm coming to her, so I'm happy I kept this to myself. On the other hand, if my dreams often came true, I probably would have treated this with more reverence, finding a way to warn her without terrifying her in the process.

Spirit Guides and Guardians

Everybody has spirit guides, but not everyone is aware of them. They could be there, whispering in your mind, guiding you throughout the day. I didn't believe in them until I experienced it firsthand. I was driving along a highway when the image of my late grandmother popped into my head, telling me to slow down. Seconds later, my front tire blew out. If I hadn't slowed down, I probably would've been badly injured if not killed.

Find your guides through meditation or just ask for a sign that they are there, and then follow your instincts. Sometimes your guides are those little voices in your mind urging you to make a decision. Listen to them and see what happens.

Document Everything

Keep a journal to write down the things that come to you. Did you have a strange dream that a friend was going to have a difficult pregnancy? Did you get an odd feeling when you met a co-worker for the first time? Being able to go back and track this is helpful for psychic growth. Make sure to record the date, time of day and although they seem trivial, the small things, like the mood you were in, the moon cycle and the weather. You may discover there is a pattern to your abilities.

Research

It took me a long time to trust that my feelings were much more than just my imagination. I read every book I could get my hands on, and took several psychic awareness classes. Every piece of information brought me closer to understanding my abilities. My experiences will probably be different from yours. Use this as a guide to learn more about your own capabilities, but don't look at it as an instruction manual. Wisdom often comes from numerous sources. Never stop learning. Read everything you can and attend classes when you get the chance.

Share Your Experiences

Most people are afraid to talk about these things. They're scared that other people are going to make fun of them or think they're crazy, when in truth many other people have these feelings as well. Find someone you can trust to talk about it. If possible, find someone who is going through a similar situation, or someone who has mastered the skill you want to develop. Finding a good tutor could make the difference between wondering and understanding.

Everyone is Different

Several of my friends are also sensitives. They know when a ghost or spirit enters a room, but their cues are different. Just because you don't feel the same cues, doesn't mean you aren't experiencing something. Use your abilities to help one another grow and develop.

Using Pets for Validation

I often noticed my cats look at the doorway when I felt a ghost come into the room. I began watching them closely, wondering if they were seeing or hearing the same thing I was. While there aren't any hard facts to support the concept that dogs and cats can see ghosts, it has been documented that they have much keener senses, which makes me wonder what they are capable of seeing.

A cat's vision is different from ours. It's geared towards movement to assist them in hunting, also allowing them to see better in low light situations. Cats also have a better grasp on colors at the red end of the spectrum, allowing them to differentiate between blues and violets better than we can.

Many paranormal investigators use full spectrum cameras on investigations. These cameras photograph a broader array of the color spectrum than what can be seen with human eyes, often capturing strange shapes and anomalies in the photos. Is this what our pets are seeing?

Animals also can hear much better than we can. A dog can detect sounds well beyond the spectrum of human hearing. While humans typically hear sounds from 12Hz to 20,000 Hz, a dog can hear nearly four times greater, in the 40Hz to 60,000 Hz range. If you don't believe this, just blow on a dog whistle or download an app on your smart phone to test it yourself.

When I tried this, I was dismayed to discover that I could only hear up to 12,000 Hz, but when I pressed the button at the 20,000 Hz range, every pet in my house sat up and looked at me. Is it possible that spirit communication transpires in a frequency that is either above or below our range of hearing?

Many people speculate that ghostly phenomena exists at a different plane of existence. Researchers collecting EVP's (Electronic Voice Phenomena) will often record spirit responses on digital recorders that the human ear cannot hear at the time of the recording. You will not hear a true EVP response at the time you ask your questions, but the answers get captured on a digital recorder, suggesting that spirit communication is conducted at a higher or lower range of the audible spectrum. This is something we as humans can't hear, but our pets may be able to hear. The next time you get a cue that a ghost is nearby, watch your pets to see how they react. It could be affirming.

Practice Makes Perfect

Talk to other people about what they are feeling, but don't expect someone to hand you a magic wand that makes you a sensitive overnight. You will have to figure some things out on your own.

Unlocking this sixth sense could change your life in many ways. It is a matter of taking a natural gift and exercising it until you've built it into a powerful asset.

Joni wrote *The Soul Collector* after experiencing a horrific paranormal experience.

Be Prepared

When sensitives come into contact with ghosts, it's a different situation for them than it is with non-sensitive people. Sensitives are like beacons to the spirit world. We stand out to them as bright as stadium lights in the darkness. When they see us, they often flock to us.

I didn't understand my vulnerabilities when I first began investigating. I just walked out into an invisible playing field, armed with a little bit of information, which was just enough to make me dangerous to myself.

I was intrigued by the way I could pinpoint the location of the ghosts. It helped my paranormal investigative team know where to set up their equipment. The information I pulled from the ghosts helped me ask meaningful questions during EVP sessions as well. What I didn't count on was the fact that they might start following me home.

The truth is ghosts will often follow a sensitive. Perhaps they think we can help them pass along a message to their loved ones, or cross them over to the other side. Or maybe they are just craving a human experience. Being around us makes them feel better.

Unfortunately, not every sensitive can distinguish between positive and negative entities. I hear a tone and sometimes get an impression, but this isn't always the case. Sometimes I just know a ghost is in the room. I don't always know if their intentions are good or bad. This makes them unpredictable and sometimes dangerous.

After having an extremely malevolent attachment, I'm leery of allowing anything paranormal to get too close to me; however, the ghosts don't usually stop to ask permission first. They follow me anyway.

I had another bad experience with a negative entity last year. I don't know where I picked her up. She may have followed me from the grocery store, or detected my energy as I drove past a cemetery. I just remember hearing a tone I identified as a female ghost, and I got a mind picture of a young woman with long dark hair and angry, angry eyes. I did what I usually do in these situations. I told her to leave, and then I ignored her.

After a few days, she was still there. I tried smudging the house with sage, saying prayers and firmly telling her to leave, but nothing happened. She just laughed at me as she settled in for the long haul.

Her wrath began on a Monday morning with the smell of gas. I woke up and made my way to the kitchen. I was stopped short by the overpowering smell of propane gas. It didn't take long to discover the source. One of the gas burners on my stove was turned on.

It was a curious moment for me because I was home alone. In order to turn the burner on, you have to press the button inwards and then turn it. In my eight years in the house, it was something that had never happened to me. My pets lacked opposable thumbs, so I knew they couldn't have turned it on. I hadn't cooked anything in days, either. I just shrugged and busied myself opening doors and windows to clear out the potentially dangerous fumes. The thought that it might be paranormal never entered my mind.

Two days later, something else happened to make me question it. As I walked past the bathroom, I noticed that the toilet paper roll was missing. The entire silver cylinder was also gone. I looked around in all the rooms, but couldn't find it. I initially blamed it on the cats. Even though they never did it before, it was within the realm of reason. I figured I would find it later under a bed or behind a dresser. What I wasn't expecting was to find it back in place an hour later.

I walked past the bathroom on my way to refill my coffee mug, and I happened to glance into the bathroom. What I saw stopped me dead in my tracks as I stared at the impossible sight. The toilet paper and cylinder were back in place as if they were never missing.

I took a deep breath and looked around me. I didn't see anything, but the signature tone I heard all week was even louder than before. Nothing of this magnitude had ever happened to me in this house. I've had the occasional item disappear only to reappear somewhere else later, but it was never this obvious. It would usually be something I could blame on myself, like finding my keys on the coffee table instead of in my purse where I swore I left them. There was always a possible explanation. This time, there wasn't one. Toilet paper rolls simply don't disappear and then reappear back where they were in the beginning.

As I stood there trying very hard not to allow fear to overcome me, I couldn't help but wonder. What else was she capable of? If she could move toilet paper, could she move knives, as well? Could she push me down the stairs or harm one of my pets? I suddenly remembered the gas incident from days before. Was she responsible for that, too?

I knew to stifle my fear, but it wasn't easy. Fear feeds them, giving them a deep-dish serving of the energy they need to be more active. I probably don't have to explain how hard this is to do. Fear is our first natural reaction to unsettling incidents. Running and screaming would be the second and third reactions. I took another deep breath and continued down the hallway to refill my coffee, trying not to think too much.

Over the course of the next few days, I began to feel her more clearly. Her anger was so powerful, it was almost visible, radiating with spiked thorns every time she came near me. I tried to quiet my mind and ask her what she wanted, but all I got was a sense of overwhelming anger. She was either really mad at me, or I reminded her of someone who had wronged her during her life. I tried to reason with her, but she just would not go away.

I reached out to my spirit guides and guardians. I asked for help and heard one swoop in quickly.

The night was filled with the sounds of them moving around my room. I could imagine them fighting as the sounds grew louder and then softer as they continued to battle. By the next morning, all was quiet. My guardians had won the war.

I was safe.

I've had several close calls since then, but nothing compared to what I experienced with the Soul Collector. If you haven't read my book about my experience with him, I hope you give it a read. It's a good example of the dangers that sensitives can experience when they are ill-prepared.

Protection from Others

Other living people can also affect your energy, whether it is intentional or not. Those people can be like psychic vampires for a sensitive, either altering your energy with theirs or stealing your energy altogether.

Grounding and shielding can be effective depending on the circumstances. Sometimes, just removing yourself from the person is measure enough. Working with a mentor can help you defend yourself against this.

(Above)The author poses with the Ghost Adventures crew as they set up to investigate at the Haunted Victorian Mansion in April 2013.

Protecting Yourself during a Paranormal Investigation

If you are a sensitive who is also a paranormal investigator, you'll need to take more precautions with protection than a non-sensitive. Understand the extent of your abilities. An intelligent haunting will require different protection than a demonic possession. Some hauntings, such as a demonic possession or a negative intelligent ghost, should be handled by people with more experience in these matters. Don't subject yourself to a situation you can't manage.

Before you go on an investigation, also make sure the people you are investigating with are like-minded. I cannot say enough about this. Avoid groups who employ an aggressive stance on spirit and ghost interaction. If you have never investigated with them before, ask a few important questions first.

Provoking

Provoking is used by some investigators to illicit a response from the ghosts around them. They will use rough language or tone of voice to demand that the ghosts respond to them. My feelings are that it's wrong. You are going into some else's environment and should always be respectful. Would you go into someone's house and put your finger on his chest and demand that he talks to you?

It also puts you in a position where you could be angering a ghost that has already been pushed past its limit. The results could be devastating. The ghost could lash out with violence, providing the provoker with more than he or she can handle. Ask the leader of the group how they feel about provoking before you investigate with them. As a sensitive, you can't risk putting yourself in danger for the sake of a good EVP or ghost response. It's just not worth it.

Respecting Their Space

Some ghosts don't want to be bothered. If you ask them if they want you to leave and they say "yes," then you should respect that and get out of there immediately.

We have investigated locations where I have felt unwelcomed. As a sensitive, this is just something you feel or know. Always respect the message that comes to your mind. If someone in your group feels this way, listen to them, as well.

We were once investigating at a location that saw a great deal of investigations over the past year. It was clear to me that they were tired of all the questions and just wanted to be left alone. Even though we were prepared to spend several hours there, I moved my team to another area in the house to get away from the weary ghosts in that area. We found that the ghosts on another floor were more comfortable talking with us, which worked out well for everyone involved, living and dead.

Listen to your team members, too. While we were at another haunted location, I wasn't getting the same message as another sensitive. I felt calm and secure, but she was getting the distinct impression that we needed to leave. I didn't ask any questions. I just packed up and left. The next day, the location was investigated again by another team and someone got scratched. This reinforced my belief to always listen to your gut. If you or someone else in your group feels as though you need to leave an area, listen to the message. Before you investigate with a team, ask them how they feel about this. It could make a big difference in how the investigation goes for you. Are they there to help ghosts, or to help the living deal with ghosts? Or are they just there to get a thrill or find evidence to show off to their friends?

Before the Investigation

The methods of protecting yourself during an investigation are varied and diverse. Some people will use all of these suggestions, while others will pick and choose from the list.

I recommend finding something that works for you and sticking with it. Being consistent is essential for developing routines. It's easy to forgo protection or forget it in the excitement of the moment, but it's not something you want to neglect. It's almost like driving a car without insurance. You may drive 50,000 miles and not get into an accident, but this doesn't mean you'll never have something happen. You can't predict the future. If you come in contact with a negative entity, make sure you protect yourself against the negative energy. I learned this the hard way and will never forget it again.

State of Mind

Always be in a good state of mind. If you are depressed, tired or not in a good place, don't go. You are more susceptible to ghost attachment with your resistance down.

When I encountered the Soul Collector, I was in a very bad place in my life. I was depressed and sad after a long-term relationship suddenly ended. When my friends invited me to go on an investigation, I was eager to have something to do to take my mind off my troubles. As it turns out, this was the last thing I should have done. When you have low energy, either physically or mentally, you become more vulnerable to ghost attachment. It limits the amount of energy you emit for protecting yourself, essentially making your shield ineffective. Although I went to the area many times before and was able to protect myself, going in a lesser state of mind made me a prime candidate for him.

Prayer

Prayer is an effective tool for many situations. People with long-term ailments have used it to help them recover. People with problems use it to find strength. Sensitives can use it, too.

Your personal belief system will dictate which prayer you use. I will suggest a few, but you should use what resonates with you.

> **Prayer of Protection**
> The Light of God surrounds me.
> The Love of God enfolds me.
> The Power of God protects me.
> The Presence of God watches over me.
> The Mind of God guides me.
> The Life of God flows through me.
> The Laws of God direct me.
> The Power of God abides within me.
> The Joy of God uplifts me.
> The Strength of God renews me.
> The Beauty of God inspires me.
> Wherever I am, God is!
> Amen

Another favorite among investigators is the Saint Michael's Prayer. We often use this.

> **Saint Michael's Prayer**
> Saint Michael the Archangel, defends us in battle;
> be our protection against the wickedness and snares of the devil.
> May God rebuke him, we humbly pray;
> and do though, O Prince of the heavenly host, by the power of God, thrust into hell Satan and all the evil spirits who prowl about the world seeking the ruin of souls.
> Amen

Medallions or Religious Symbols

A medallion that makes you feel safe will help with your protection. I have a rose quartz necklace my friend Sandy made for me. I wear it all the time because it was made with good intent, and it makes me feel protected. Below are several suggestions. These are a few of the options available depending on your faith or belief system.

Types of Medallions or Religious Symbols
• Cross or Crucifix
• Saint Michael's Medallion
• Saint Benedict's Medallion
• Wiccan Star Pentagram
• Celtic Symbol
• Crystal

Protection Stones

Many people feel that some stones carry protective properties. They have been used since the dawn of time for various purposes. Some stones, such as rose quartz, help improve your heart and mind balance, making you more open to give and receive love. Other stones, such as hematite, are grounding stones. They help you turn frantic energy into calming energy. I often carry both of these stones in my pocket and use them as my "touch stones" to help me in times of stress or unrest.

You can find stones online, but I feel that it's always better to visit a metaphysics shop to pick these out yourself. Weigh them in your hand and see how they feel. The right stone will call to you and you'll know which one will help you the most.

Some people believe unpolished stones hold more energy than polished stones. Do your research to discover which stones you need. Here's a small sampling of what is available:

Protection Stones	Properties/Protection
Agate	Many different types offer different properties; overall for strength, protection, courage.
Amethyst	For peace, love, protection and banishing nightmares. Blocks stress from environmental situations.
Turquoise	One of the oldest protection stones. Has a calming, regenerative energy.
Jade	Keeps the wearer from harm while promoting harmony and good fortune.
Red Jasper	Sends negative energy back to the sender.
Jet	Absorbs negative energy and prevents nightmares.
Hematite	For grounding. Turns negative energy into useful energy.
Black Tourmaline	Absorbs negative energy. Powerful grounding stone, useful for areas of high electromagnetic energy.
Snowflake Obsidian	Protects the wearer from negative energy, while promoting peace and balance.

Cleansing and Charging Protective Stones

When you purchase new gemstones, always cleanse and recharge them. You don't know where they've been and what they've been used for, so you'll want to make sure they are neutralized and ready to work for you.

Like anything else, there are multiple methods of cleansing and charging gemstones. I prefer to simply hold them under running tap water for a minute or two, visualizing all energy washing through the stone and leaving it ready for charging. Others will recommend smudging it with sage or giving it a salt-water bath.

I also recommend doing a thorough cleansing of your stones during each full moon. Just place the stones on a windowsill that gets exposure to the moon and leave them overnight. Make sure to charge them again with your own intent the following day.

To charge a stone, you are essentially programming it for your wishes and purposes. Hold it in your hand and visualize what you would like this gemstone to do for you. When I am charging a protective stone, I simply think to myself, "Please keep me protected from any energy that is not my own."

You can use gemstones for a variety of purposes besides protection. I have a citrine stone I like to keep beside my laptop. Citrine is very effective for promoting creativity. When I'm feeling like I could use a little help I hold the stone and admire its beauty. Inspiration soon comes to me.

Pick which stones to use each day. I keep my gemstones in an open bowl in my bedroom. When I get dressed every morning, I choose the ones I want to use for that day. I might mix rose quartz with hematite, and add black tourmaline. This mix will keep me emotionally balanced and protected, no matter what comes my way. Experiment with this to find what works for you.

Protection Spray

Containing essential oils and fragrances, such as rosemary, myrrh, cedar wood and frankincense, protection sprays help ward off negative energy. They are readily available from many different sellers online. Remember the smell as you investigate and don't mistake it as a sign from the spirits.

I use this on myself before and after investigations. I spray a little on the top of my head s I visualize it protecting me from negative energy. I also use it to cleanse my house periodically. Since I live in a situation where I can't burn sage, I use protective sprays instead, spritzing them into all the corners of the rooms, as well as in front of windows and doorways. It leaves a nice scent in the room and chases away all the negative energy. I typically do this weekly or as needed.

Sage

Often referred to as smudging, burning sage began as a Native American ritual for cleansing and blessing people and places. It changes the energy and alters the vibration level, which leaves the space in better harmony.

White sage is my favorite. You can mix it with sweet grass or cedar. While burning the sage, take turns allowing the smoke to cover member of the group completely. Start with the bottom of your feet, working upwards, making sure to cover the front and the back of the person. When closing an investigation, you should also sage your equipment.

Like the protection spray, you can use it in your house and car, too. Do this before an investigation to surround yourself with good, pure energy. It's always a good way to start an investigation.

Sea Salt

Sea salt has powerful protective properties. People have used it throughout the ages to prevent negative energy from entering a space. I have seen investigators make circles around their vehicles or homes with this. Others draw lines at the doorways and windows. The theory is that spirits cannot pass across the salt. I often use it in cleansing baths, as well.

Grounding

Grounding before an investigation is essential. You should always begin an investigation with a calm mindset. Push away all those negative energies, and allow yourself to start strong and relaxed. I probably ground myself a dozen times a day. It helps remove stress and negative emotions from my body and mind. I do this before ghost hunts, but especially afterwards.

Shielding

While I do this every morning as a protective precaution, I always put more effort into reinforcing my shield before an investigation, especially if I'm going to an unknown location. When you go to places like cemeteries, you never know what you're going to encounter. There can be a real mix of good and bad energy. It's best to prepare for the worst. I always take a minute after I've grounded myself to visualize my protective shield around me, standing strong and secure. This can be a very useful tool for keeping you protected from ghost attachment during the investigation.

Spirit Guides and Guardians

Your spirit guides and guardians can help keep you protected, too. It's like having a second line of defense to keep you safe. A spirit guide or guardian could be family members or friends who have passed on. Or they could be guardians who were assigned to protect you. Reach out to them and ask for their protection.

I discovered one of my spirit guides through a guided mediation.

I am not necessarily good at sitting still for long moments, which can be both a blessing and a curse. I found that using a guided mediation video from the Internet was helpful in keeping me tuned into what I was supposed to be doing instead of making grocery lists and stressing about the things I hadn't done yet during the day.

During the mediation, when I got to a place of deep relaxation, I asked for my spirit guide to present him or herself. I was treated to a visual image of a woman. She looked very angelic, but strong. I asked for her name, and she gave it to me. I often call to her in times of stress and always feel her presence. I also feel the presence of relatives who have passed on, and I often call to them, too.

Psychic Mediums

Having a comfortable relationship with a reputable psychic medium is a useful asset for a sensitive. Before you go into any situation, consider the worst possible scenario, and then plan for it. A good psychic medium can help you do this. Make sure this person is available for you before, during, and after an investigation.

It took me a while to find someone who was a good fit for me, but it was worth the effort. Whenever I encounter a situation I can't handle on my own, I reach out to her for assistance. She also offers advice on advancing my abilities. To find this person for yourself, start by asking the people around you if they know someone. A personal recommendation is far better than picking someone from a list on the Internet.

During the Investigation

- Be respectful during the investigation, ensuring your questions aren't rude and offensive during EVP sessions. Would you ask a total stranger a personal question? Then you shouldn't ask it of the dead, either. Some ghosts don't know they are dead. Always keep this in mind during your investigations and treat them like you would like to be treated yourself.
- Don't ask ghosts to touch you. Unless you are capable of pushing them off, don't allow them to get any closer than an arm's length from you. You don't want them going home with you.
- Don't offer to let the ghosts use your energy. This goes back to allowing them into your space. If you aren't capable of pushing them off, don't invite them near you. If they use your energy, you'll find yourself feeling drained for days. It's just not worth the risk.
- Don't go anywhere alone. Always travel in groups of two or more. If someone gets injured, the other person can get help. In addition, if you see or hear something paranormal, it's always helpful to have a witness.
- Respect your team's wishes. While investigating, many people prefer a scientific approach to investigating. They capture evidence used to validate the haunting. Personally, I find it annoying if a sensitive frequently interrupts the investigation to tell us what he or she is feeling. It often leads the team in an entirely different direction, sometimes following inaccurate information. I would rather compare notes afterwards to see if we were having similar feelings.
- Skip the initial tour, so you aren't tainted by the stories regarding the location. If you notice something relevant, it'll be more validating for you and your team.

- Keep your impressions to yourself until after each session ends. Write it down if necessary, so you'll remember.
- Always close communications sessions, Like spirit box or EVP sessions, for example, when you're finished by telling the ghosts and spirits that you're ending communication with them, and that they must remain where they are.

(Above) An example of a shadow person. This dark profile appeared suddenly on the homeowner's television set. A cleansing was performed several days later and the entity was removed.

Photo courtesy of George Brun

After the Investigation

- Do a closing prayer of your choice. We often recite the St. Michael's prayer again.
- Burn sage. Move it around each investigator and sage your equipment and vehicles as well. This helps cleanse the air and increase the harmony.
- Grounding is helpful at this time, too.
- Tell the spirits they can't follow you. Tell them their feet are firmly grounded where they are.
- Don't linger at the investigation site. As soon as you've ended the investigation, get moving. You don't want to give anyone a second chance to tag along.
- Bathe when you get home. Some people shower, but I always prefer to take a bath with a touch of sea salt to wash off any residue of the investigation. I also cleanse my protection stones at the same time and then recharge them with my intent to stay protected.
- Eat something healthy, and then get a good night's sleep. This fortifies you and helps rebuild your energy. Investigations are often quite draining, but half the battle for staying protected during an investigation is taking good care of yourself. If your energy is high, you will be far less attractive to ghost attachment. They would rather pursue an easier target. While many ghosts are firmly attached to a location and have no desire to follow you, it's still important to be careful. You'll never know which ones are rooted in place and which ones will follow you until you leave the location.
- Have faith. Don't allow doubt to weaken everything you've done to stay protected. Doubt is like dropping a vase, and then gluing it back together again. It may still hold water, but it will probably leak.

Paranormal Hangovers

Paranormal investigators often experience a sensation after investigations that we call a paranormal hangover. It's a feeling of utter exhaustion, lack of concentration and a strong need for rest. There are many theories on why this happens.

Some of it could be due to a change in your sleep pattern. Instead of going to sleep at your normal time, ghost hunters often stay up late, not retiring until the early hours of the morning. Other contributing factors could be physical exhaustion, or from subjecting yourself to excess temperature ranges, depending on the season.

I believe the main reason for a paranormal hangover is from energy thieves.

(Above) The author's niece at the Haunted Victorian Mansion. The author saw the light as she snapped the photo and ruled out factors that may have contributed to the image being a reflection.

Photo by the author

Ghosts need energy to communicate. Many ghost hunting teams bring EMF pumps to investigations, which they believe creates a field of electromagnetic energy to give the ghosts an energy boost, so they can better communicate. Others have reported great results with this device, but I've never noticed a tremendous difference myself. What I do see is the ghosts using our energy.

Ever have a location that truly calls out to you? You want to go back again and again, but you can't figure out why. I have my own theory on this. They're calling to you because they're hungry. You return to the location, have a great investigation, but then you feel drained afterwards. This is because they were using your energy to help them communicate, leaving you feeling as though you have been sucked dry.

(Above) The Houghton Mansion in North Adams, Massachusetts

Photo by the author

One of my favorite locations to investigate is the Houghton Mansion in North Adams, Massachusetts. I have investigated there four times over the course of the past five years. Every time I visit, I come home feeling absolutely drained. It took me a while to understand what was happening to me.

Being a sensitive, the ghosts are usually happy to talk to me and the Houghton Mansion is no exception. I always capture an amazing amount of evidence there. It is as if the ghosts line up, fighting each other for the opportunity to communicate with me. The last time I was there, I saw a partial apparition dart across the basement. The basement is supposedly haunted by a little girl. The apparition I saw, which was confirmed by Marian Luoma, another investigator, looked like the bottom of a small girl's dress.

In order for the ghosts to do this, they need a tremendous amount of energy. Judging by the way I felt the next few days, I was pretty sure they got it from me.

To prevent a paranormal hangover, try these tips:

- Always ground yourself thoroughly before and after each investigation. Allow the negative energy to flow through your body and into the ground. This leaves you in a better position to protect yourself.
- Shielding is important during investigations. It prevents ghosts from getting too close to you. If you find that you're still feeling weak and exhausted after an investigation, this may be a sign that your shields aren't working at full capacity. Go back to the visualizations and work on building your shield. You can work with a psychic medium to help reinforce it.
- Protection prayers are important, as well. If you're feeling drained, ask for help. Whether it's a religious prayer or a

conversation you're having with your guides or guardians, ask them to keep you shielded from energy vampires.
- As stated before, never tell ghosts they can use your energy, and never invite them to touch you. You are only asking for trouble when you do this, and you pose the risk of being used for more than just your energy.

Recovering from a paranormal hangover is similar to recovering from an alcohol-induced hangover. Here are some effective ways to feel better faster:

- Get enough rest afterwards. If you stayed out until four in the morning and didn't get into bed until six, then it stands to reason that you'll need to sleep until one or two in the afternoon. Many people can't do this since it interferes with their internal body clocks. The best thing to do is to sleep as long as you can, and then get up and make the best of it.
- Keeping yourself hydrated will help keep you more attentive and alert. Avoid consuming too much caffeinated beverages, since caffeine can act as a diuretic, causing you to dehydrate even further. Drink plenty of water instead.
- Get out and stay busy. When faced with a paranormal hangover, most people just want to vegetate on the sofa in front of the television all day. While it does help kill the time, it won't help you recover. Get out and enjoy the sunshine and fresh air. You'll be amazed at how much better you feel.
- Eat a balanced diet and load up on protein. Our bodies crave protein when we are energy depleted. Proteins, such as lean meats, nuts, cheese and eggs can provide you with a boost to help you recover.
- Stay away from refined sugars and processed, salty foods. I always crave soda and chips when I'm feeling energy depleted, but neither serves to help me regain my energy.

Wholesome foods like green leafy vegetables, fruits high in Vitamin C, and plenty of water are your best allies for regaining your energy.

- I also find that investigating often disrupts my normal sleep pattern, leaving me off schedule for several days later. I combat this by taking a melatonin supplement before bedtime on a daily basis. I've found that 5 milligrams works well for me, but always check with your doctor to find out the correct dosage. It will vary from person to person.
- Go to bed on time the day after an investigation. Fight the urge to nap during the day. This will only prevent you from getting to sleep later when it's your normal bedtime. Avoid watching television or using a computer for several hours prior to bedtime, as well as caffeine. Everyone is affected differently by caffeine. I've found that if I avoid it after two in the afternoon, I'm usually fine by the time I retire for bed at ten in the evening.

(Above) Photo of a possible outdoor vortex. The investigator confirmed no one was smoking and it wasn't due to warm breath on a cold night.

Photo courtesy of George Brun

What to Do if Something Follows You

This is every sensitive's worst nightmare, and it is something you should know how to handle should it happen to you.

Claim Ownership

Let them know they need to move on. Tell them to look for the white light, which is a doorway to the other side. Also, tell them to reach out to one of their family members who has already passed on to help them make the transition. Being dead on our side of the veil is an unpleasant experience. Although ghosts can see and hear the things we do, they have limited abilities. If this doesn't work, move onto the next tip.

Arrange a House Blessing

Most religious leaders are happy to bless your home providing you are a member of their church. Having the backing of the church behind them can make a difference. If the ghost was once human, this is something they will remember from their living days and they may trust it more than if you cleansed your house yourself.

Use a Trusted Psychic Medium

Reach out to a psychic medium to cleanse your house. They can often break through the language barrier and get the message through more clearly. Some psychic mediums will do this for free, while others will charge for their services. This isn't a time to skimp. Finding the best medium available will save you time and energy later.

Cleanse the House Yourself

This is a good first step and may be enough to solve the issue. Ghosts don't always understand they can't come with you. When you claim your space, it lets them know they can't just move in with you on a whim.

1. Before you begin, open a few windows in your house.
2. Light a stick of white sage mixed with sweet grass that you purchased from your local metaphysical shop or online. If you can't use sage, you can use protection spray or spray holy water on every wall, window, and doorway. Be calm but firm as you do this and ask your spirit guides or guardians to help you.
3. Fill every room in your house with the smoke, starting with the outermost corner, working your way to the front of the house. Let the sage smoke cover every inch of space in every room, from floor to ceiling. Some say the smoke is calming to them, helping them transition to the next plane.
4. As you burn the sage, tell them you're filling the house with light and love, and that no negative energy can remain. Tell them this is your house and you are taking it back. Encourage them to find the peace and love they desire through the white light. Tell them it's time for them to go. Some people will say a prayer as well.
5. When you are finished, extinguish the sage stick on the front walkway.
6. Cut your ties. You can do this physically, as well as mentally. Cut the cords that connect you to this energy, and then move on. Don't think about it. Shove it out of your mind. Thinking about it could actually draw them back in, so avoid this as much as possible.

Some people follow this up with a ring of sea salt around the border of the house. If this isn't feasible, sprinkle it on the windowsills and doorsteps. This seals the property and prevents negative energy from returning.

Others will also take a warm bath filed with sea salt and lavender, to cleanse their body of the energy.

What do you do if your house is still paranormally active after you've taken all these measures? Some ghosts are resistant about moving on, so the typical measures aren't going to work with them. It's time to move to a second phase.

- Contact a trusted psychic medium, if you haven't already done so. There may be more going on than you know. If the ghost is advanced and is negative, you don't want to handle this by yourself, especially not the first time. Find someone who has experience removing negative energy. While demonic activity is rare, it's something that should be handled by someone with expertise. An experienced psychic medium will be able to determine the type of haunting and help you find the correct measures to deal with it.
- Research the history of the house. Go to your local town hall and look at the census records and death records to find out if the ghost is a former resident of the home. Sometimes a tragic event could have caused them to stay behind. Or maybe they're just attached to the house. Sometimes just knowing what you're dealing with helps move them on to the other side.
- Do nothing. Allow the energy to calm down on its own. Don't acknowledge them and don't be fearful. Just go about your life as usual. Sometimes this simple action makes a difference, but sometimes it can make it worse.
- The last resort, which I don't think is a good one, is to move. I don't like this last option, because you are only leaving the problem for someone else to deal with. Or worse, you go through the effort of moving, only to discover the ghost has followed you.

Always keep in mind that ghosts were people too, and not everything is going to work with every ghost. The more resistant a ghost is, the harder they are to move along. Always start at the beginning of the list and rule out normal explanations first. You will save yourself a lot of time and stress. When I went through this myself back in the 1990's, I wasn't sure what to do and the resources weren't as prevalent as they are today. I ended up moving out, leaving the energy for someone else to contend with afterwards. I later learned that the house was sold five times in five years, and it made me feel very guilty for not pursuing it further.

Whatever you do, do it with purpose and remain calm. Fear is never a good tool for working with ghosts, and neither is anger. Most hauntings are human in nature and a sense of compassion is your best ally.

What if the haunting isn't human?

When we talk about a non-human haunting, we are usually talking about a demonic situation. While these are rarer than television and movies lead us to believe, they do exist.

Signs of a non-human haunting will range from foul smells in the house and abrupt personality changes to unexplained scratches on the body. Demons don't possess locations, they possess people. They only hang out at a location to stalk the perfect victim.

The stages of a demonic possession are as follows:

- Infestation is the initial stage when the demon attaches itself to you. This is the best time to get rid of it. Once it moves to the next stage, it becomes far more difficult.
- Oppression is the way it makes you feel. It oppresses you, making you depressed, and less capable of fighting it off.

- Possession is the final step. When it's at this stage, drastic measures are necessary to get rid of it.

If you suspect your haunting isn't human, find a professional to help you. I would recommend a combination of efforts. Seek out a trusted psychic medium, as well as a member of clergy. The medium will help act as a go between, letting the others know what is going on. A member of clergy, preferably a Roman Catholic Priest, will conduct an exorcism. Don't allow someone to perform this unless they have a proven track record. This isn't the time for someone to be learning a skill, especially if your life is at stake

Always believe it will work.

Faith and a firm sense of belief will carry you much further than doubt and fear.

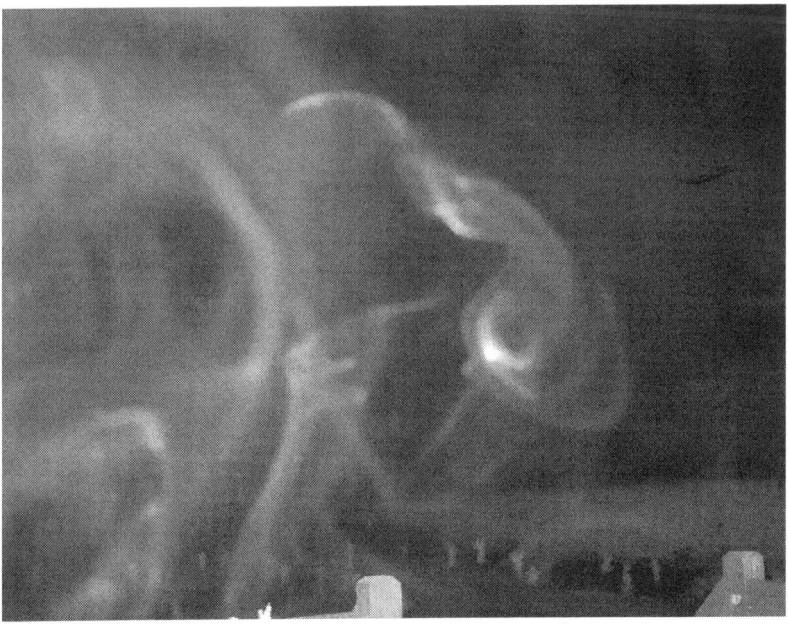

(Above) A photo taken outdoors. The investigator confirmed that no one was smoking and it wasn't due to warm breath on a cold night. See the hand in the middle? (photo courtesy of George Brun)

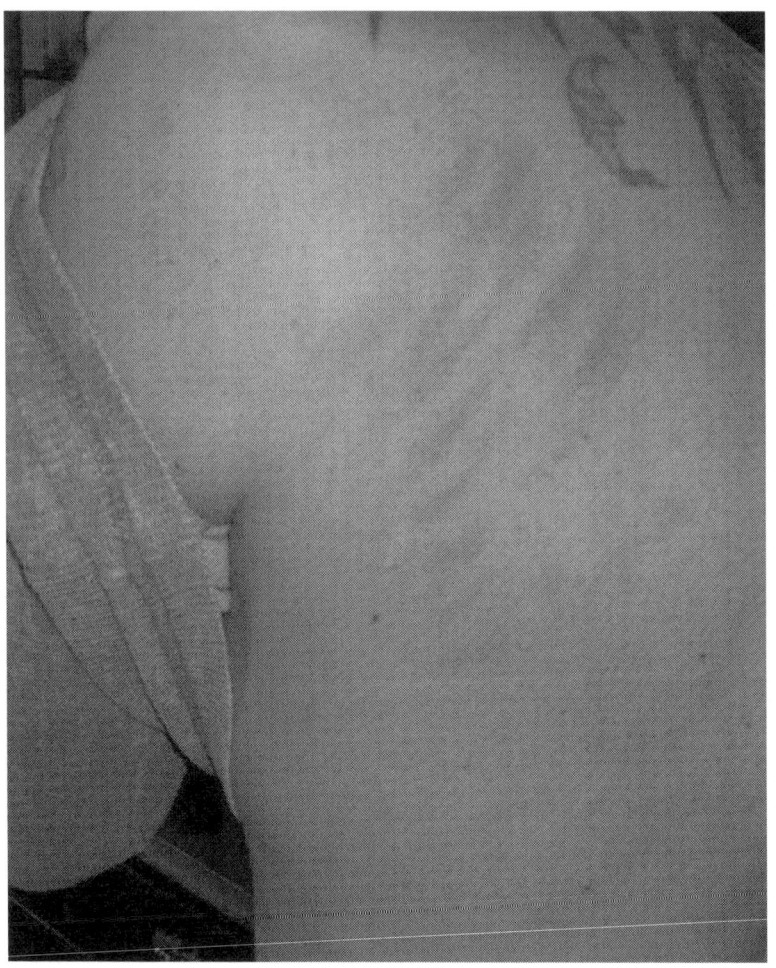

(Above) Scratches that mysteriously appeared on an investigator's back during a paranormal investigation.

Photo courtesy of George Brun

Knowing Your Limitations

We all have to start somewhere. That is how we learn and grow. However, when it comes to the paranormal, you should never put yourself in a position where you are relying on hope alone to carry you through.

A negative entity or a demonic possession is well beyond the grasp of a sensitive just coming into his or her abilities. If nothing else, you will act as bait for them, giving them an even better option for a ghostly attachment.

I learned this the hard way. After dealing with the Soul Collector, my abilities grew stronger. I began reaching out to various mediums and energy workers, learning how to protect myself. In the process, I picked up a few tricks. I learned how to cross ghosts over to the other side.

I thought this was the solution for many of my problems but it wasn't. Every time I went anywhere, ghosts began following me home. They identified me as someone who had abilities, something that grew even worse after I learned how to cross over souls. It was as if a ghostly bulletin was sent out to every ghost in the vicinity. No matter where I went, someone followed me.

A friend asked me if I could come to her house and see if she had a ghost. She was feeling ill at ease over the past few days. She felt as though she was being watched. Items kept disappearing and reappearing in other spots, and her dog began to growl at the corners of the rooms.

I went in, hopeful that I could identify it and then cross it over, but that wasn't the case. Not all ghosts are ready to be helped to the other side. Some of them actually like it here. Others still feel as though they have unfinished business to attend to first. The result was predictable. The ghost just followed me home.

I began to feel like I had a line that started at my door, running miles down the road, with ghosts all lined up, waiting to be crossed over. I had to put a stop to this, or else I would face a horrific future.

That is when I began learning how to ground and shield myself. It doesn't work all the time. Some of them still get through my shields. When I can't move them off by normal means, I always reach out to my psychic medium friend for assistance.

I recommend proceeding slowly. Don't be the only sensitive on the team until you are capable of handling the ramifications. If you investigate with a psychic medium, you will be protected better, and you'll have the opportunity to acquire more knowledge.

Without knowing everything that's transpiring at a haunted location, you could find yourself making serious mistakes. Some locations with old hauntings might have a peace keeper ghost in residence. This soul keeps the others in line, while preventing more ghosts from moving in. If you mindlessly go in and cross this soul over, you risk leaving chaos behind. While I'm a firm believer that anyone who wants to cross over should have that opportunity, I also feel that you should always know the full story before you proceed. This is why it's good to have a psychic medium with you.

Learning how to protect yourself is crucial for a sensitive. If you don't believe this, continue reading the preview of The Soul Collector below. Ghost hunting isn't always fun and games. Sometimes, it can be deadly.

Joni Mayhan is an experienced paranormal investigator and author. To learn more, please check out her website: Jonimayhan.com

Please continue reading for a preview of The Soul Collector – One Paranormal Investigator's Worst Nightmare. *Now available on Amazon.com for Kindle or paperback.*

The Soul Collector

By

Joni Mayhan

Chapter 1

I was warned to never talk about him.

I was supposed to just walk away and forget the entire experience, totally erasing him from my memory. If I didn't, there was a very good chance he could come back to find me again. I held onto this story for several years, trying to follow their advice, but I just couldn't.

I needed to tell my story.

I wasn't in a very good place when he found me. I was at the end of a two-year relationship with someone I thought I would spend the rest of my life with, growing old together. When he walked away so suddenly, it left my whole life in shambles.

With my entire family living a thousand miles away, I didn't have anyone to turn to. I'm not the kind of person who cries to other people about her problems. I swallowed the pain whole, and then allowed it to consume me. It burrowed and spread, reaching into every cell of my being, leaving me nothing more than a shell.

I was forty-seven years old, living in a small house in the rural town of Barre, Massachusetts. I had purchased the nine-hundred square foot ranch house after my divorce in 2005, hoping to find a place to lick my wounds before moving onto my happily-ever-after. Six years later, I was still in the same place with no hope in sight.

After spending weeks locked inside my house with the curtains drawn, I finally decided to get out and do something. People told me that staying busy was the best cure for a broken heart, so I tried.

A friend invited me to go ghost hunting. As it turns out, it was the worst thing I could have done. It brought me to the Soul Collector.

(Below: Joni investigating in the basement of one of her favorite haunted locations.

Chapter 2

I got into ghost hunting quite by accident.

I spent a solid three years after my divorce hiding out in my house. I didn't have any friends to speak of and had nowhere to go. Besides, people were hurtful and scary. I preferred spending the time with my pets or by myself, writing, reading, and watching movies.

Sometimes I feel like a hopeless cause. I've never been socially adept. Since grade school, I've had a difficult time interacting with my peers. Being small as a child, I was often picked on by schoolyard bullies. I didn't fare much better in high school. It seemed like every time I allowed myself to get close to someone, I ended up getting hurt. In the end, I decided it was better to just be alone and save myself the pain. It turned out to be a lonely decision that I would soon reconsider.

The one friend I retained into adulthood was actually an old high-school boyfriend who still lived in Indiana. Finding ourselves both single after years of marriage, we forged a long-distance friendship. John was the one who got me to come out of my shell. First, he talked me into setting up an online dating profile.

Initially, I was almost giddy with all the attention I was suddenly getting. After going for days without seeing another soul, I was being invited out onto dates with eligible men. John was doing the same thing back in Indiana and we started using one another as sounding boards.

"I need a woman's point of view," he'd say, then ask me a question. I'd offer my best advice, eventually helping him connect with his soon-to-be wife Melinda. I'd run situations and concerns past him for a man's point of view. We spent many long nights on the phone just chatting and helping each other through the hard times.

"You need to get out of your house," he told me one day. "Why don't you look into Meetup.com? Find something you like on there." He'd found a kayaking group there and enjoyed the occasional weekend outing with a group of people who shared his love of the water. He suggested I look into it to see if I could find a ghost hunting group, knowing how much I was into the paranormal.

While I had never investigated before, I was well versed on the subject. I'd spent the past few years amassing quite a collection of books on the paranormal. I read them from cover to cover, over and over again. I understood the difference between a residual haunting and an intelligent spirit. I was intrigued by the concept of EVPs, and even had my own digital recorder to record spirit voices. It was time to put my knowledge to work.

I took John's advice and quickly found a paranormal meet-up group. I signed up for their next event and waited eagerly for the day to arrive.

The first event was a wash out. The people who ran the event were a flaky bunch. They set up a meet-up at the Hoosic Tunnel in North Adams, Massachusetts.

Spanning over five miles, the tunnel snakes through the base of the Berkshire Mountains, cutting a path that was paved by bloodshed and death. People who dared enter it sometimes found themselves in the company of ghosts. Other people were smart enough not to walk several miles into a tunnel where an active train tunnel runs.

I had no doubt that the tunnel contained residual energy. The ground and stone have a tendency to absorb the vibrations from traumatic events in the past, replaying them like a movie, over and over again. A good example of this is Gettysburg. You can't walk out onto a battlefield without feeling the hair on the back of your neck prickle. It's as though Mother Earth is telling you, "Something happened here." People often see soldiers, or hear cannon fire, as history replays itself, but they seldom make contact with the apparitions.

While residual hauntings were interesting, making contact with an intelligent spirit was my overall goal. I had high hopes for the Hoosic Tunnel.

I brought my twenty-year-old daughter, Laura, with me to the event. We were both appropriately nervous about venturing inside. As we walked down the tracks leading to the tunnel, I could feel the anticipation rapidly turn to anxiety.

"What if a train comes?" I asked my daughter, eyeing the narrow space between the tracks and the stone walls. We might be able to press ourselves against the sides and hope for the best, but it sounded horrifically dangerous.

Laura shrugged. Suddenly, it didn't seem like such a great idea.

Several members of the meet-up group were gathered near the tunnel entrance. As we approached them, we could feel the air grow colder by several degrees.

"I'm glad to see you brought jackets," an older woman said to us. "It's quite a bit colder inside the tunnel," she said.

After quick introductions, we learned that she was the meet-up leader.

Something about her truly gave me the creeps. I wasn't sure if it was the way she looked, with her mop of unbrushed hair, or the way she was dressed in layers of skirts and shawls, accessorized by thick sandals with socks. It may have just been the wild look in her eyes that made me think of an escaped mental patient. Either way, she made me uncomfortable.

She had two other investigators with her. One was a younger woman who was the equipment expert. She walked around with an EMF meter in her hand. The other was a tall, thin man, who just stood back and watched.

"Are you getting anything?" I asked the younger woman.

"No. Nothing so far," she told me, showing me her EMF meter.

My daughter gave me a curious look, so I explained what an EMF meter does.

"It measures changes in the electro-magnetic field in an area. If a ghost comes close to us, we might see a spike in the reading," I told her. While I was anxious to have a paranormal experience, I hoped it would be a little more substantial than a blip on someone's meter.

I took my digital recorder out of my pocket and started recording, hoping for an EVP. I showed it to my daughter.

"When a ghost speaks to us, we usually can't hear them. But, if you are recording it with a digital recorder, you might record their response. It's called an EVP: electronic voice phenomena."

I asked a few questions, and then listened to the audio, hearing nothing but silence. I was disappointed, but was still hopeful. If we tried it again inside the tunnel, we might have better results.

We lingered near the entrance for several minutes. The others were milling around, talking. I was ready to go inside and get started. "Are we going in?" I finally asked.

The leader turned to look at me, her face frozen with fright. "No. I can't go in there. This place is sheer evil," she said, hopefully not noticing when I rolled my eyes.

"So, what are we going to do?" I asked, growing appropriately agitated. We paid ten dollars apiece for the experience, but we weren't going in?

"You can go in, if you want to," the leader said. "But, I'm staying right here." Her team members stuck to her side, refusing to budge as well.

I sighed and looked around, wondering what to do. It was a beautiful blue-sky day in early May. The leaves were just popping out on the trees, and the air was filled with the sweet scent of spring. We'd driven nearly two hours to be there. It seemed a shame to waste the trip only to just turn around and leave.

I turned to my daughter. "Wanna go in a little ways?" I asked.

"Might as well," she said, without much enthusiasm.

We'd spent thirteen years living in a haunted house. While we were both curious about the paranormal, we were both a little apprehensive. Sometimes opening a door to something brings you closer than you anticipated.

I'd read that ghosts often drained the batteries on your equipment, so I was well prepared for the walk. I'd put fresh batteries into four flashlights. I gave two to my daughter and kept the other two for myself. There was no way I was going to be submerged in the darkness with no light. It just wasn't going to happen.

As we were getting ready to walk in, three men joined us at the mouth of the tunnel. The oldest man was obviously the father of one of the younger men. They wanted to check out the tunnel but didn't have a flashlight. Not really thinking, I offered to let them follow us.

I should preface this with the fact that I am a little too trusting of others, at least at first. Sometimes my common sense takes a backseat to my willingness to please. It's a fault I will find myself making over and over in my life.

I walked in first, with my daughter behind me, and the three men trailing along behind us.

The tunnel was eerie. The minute we walked inside, the darkness quickly enveloped us with cold, damp fingers. I shined my light around, trying to get a feel for the place.

The tall, curved ceilings were lined with bricks. Many of the bricks had fallen, which was evident from the broken shards at our feet. Graffiti graced nearly every wall like strange artwork.

The tracks were difficult to walk on and water dripped from the ceilings, creating echoes through the tunnel. After walking for ten minutes, we were deep in the heart of the mountain. I turned around, surprised to find the tunnel opening no more than a tiny circle, floating in the darkness behind us.

It suddenly occurred to me what I was doing. I willingly led my beautiful daughter into a dark tunnel with three men I didn't know. While they seemed normal, I had no idea of their intent. My active imagination went into overdrive. What if they were bad men? I didn't think that serial killers usually hunted in packs, but who really knew?

"Ummm….you guys aren't serial killers," I said, trying to make it sound like a joke.

There was a long silence before one of the men finally spoke.

"I guess it's a little late to be asking that question, isn't it?" one of them said. He had a smile in his voice when he said it, but my discomfort level was already rising into the red zone.

"Let's turn around," I suggested, praying they wouldn't take that moment to reveal some evil personalities.

Forgetting all about my desire to do another EVP session, we turned around and made our way out of the tunnel in record time. Thankfully, the men were nothing more than true gentlemen and we parted ways at the mouth of the tunnel. I just stood there as they walked back towards the parking lot, feeling very foolish.

"What a stupid thing to do," I whispered to my daughter. I was so angry with myself for putting her in possible danger. If a train didn't run us over, the strangers could have turned out to be something other than just nice, ordinary men. What kind of mother was I?

I didn't have long to berate myself, because the meet-up leader was quickly approaching.

"Did you feel anything?" she asked, wide-eyed.

I was embarrassed she was even asking me. Admitting that I *did* or *didn't* feel something felt like social suicide. What if someone heard us? They'd think I was just as crazy as she was.

Honestly, the only thing I felt was the sense of intrigue followed by the rush of overwhelming fear. I wasn't afraid of ghosts. I was afraid of the men walking behind us and the situation I'd put us in. We nearly ran back to the car.

It would be several years later before I'd try it again.

(Below) Joni's daughter Laura, at the Hoosic Tunnel

Chapter 3

I was understandably apprehensive when I got another notification from the meet-up group. Our last event turned out to be less than expected. I wasn't sure I wanted to put myself through that again.

All I wanted was a true paranormal experience. I wanted to go on a real investigation, complete with all the tools of the trade. I wanted to play with an EMF detector, and then watch the numbers rise as a spirit approached. I longed to take part in an actual EVP session, listening to my recorded audio later, hearing the whispered voices of the dead. Mostly though, I wanted answers to my life-long questions of ghosts.

I think that everyone who gets into the field of paranormal investigating does so out of curiosity. There's just so much we don't know about the world around us. We walk through our world expecting everything to always be normal and sane, but sometimes we run into things that make us stop and think. I'd had my fair share of these moments and I wanted some of my questions answered.

I took a deep breath and signed up for the event, hoping it would end up different than my first ghost hunting experience.

I was relieved to discover that the crazy meet-up lady had left the group and was replaced by someone quite normal. Her name was Sandy MacLeod.

We were to meet in a town called Clinton, at the site of an old abandoned train tunnel.

Great, another tunnel.

I almost didn't go, but my curiosity won out in the end.

By this time, I was dating my now ex-boyfriend. While he wasn't a believer in anything supernatural, he agreed to go with me and share the experience. I was happy to have him with me. Going to something like this alone truly scared me. I had no idea what to expect.

We met Sandy in a nearby parking lot and exchanged pleasantries. She was nothing like I expected. She was a middle-aged woman with fiery red hair and glasses. Her demeanor was very calm and patient as she carefully explained what we would be doing. She looked more like a teacher than a ghost hunter. I was immediately intrigued by her.

"She seems normal," I whispered to my boyfriend.

We followed her to a roadside parking area, and then climbed up a weedy hill to a path that led to the tunnel. It was very dark that night. The moon hid behind a bank of clouds, setting the mood for the evening. Sandy gathered us in a circle and began talking about protection.

"While it's unlikely anything will follow any of us home, it doesn't hurt to take precautions," she told us. She went through a list of ways to protect ourselves, ranging from reciting prayers to cleansing the air with sage. She went on to tell us that some people carried protective medals or stones in their pockets. Others called on spirit guides or guardian angels to keep them protected.

I rolled my eyes at the mention of spirit guides. I'd heard the term before, but lumped it in with all the other mystical creatures, like unicorns and dragons. *Here we go*, I thought to myself.

"Protection also involves safety," she went on to tell us. "We never go off anywhere alone. We always go in groups."

"Even to the bathroom?" someone asked, making the group giggle.

"Well, they don't have to go in with you, but you should at least go to the area together," she said with a smile in her voice. She went onto to explain that being alone could be dangerous while investigating.

"What if one of you fell and got hurt? Or, what if you experienced something? You'd want someone there to witness it."

She sprayed us with an herbal spray that smelled faintly like pine trees and lavender, and then explained that it was a protection spray she purchased at a paranormal trade show. I just soaked it all in. I had so much to learn and was eager to get going.

We continued down the path, seeing the first hint of the tunnel emerging from the darkness. The excitement rose up in me like a small child on Christmas. I was finally going on a real ghost hunt! I couldn't have been happier.

Sandy handed out equipment for us to use, explaining each piece before turning us loose. We walked in groups, measuring the electromagnetic energy with detectors that would light up if there was a spike in energy. We walked up and down the quarter-mile train tunnel, finding very little.

Like in the Hoosic tunnel, water dripped from the ceilings and the walls were covered with graffiti. Discarded slivers of liquor bottles were mixed in with the chunky gravel, making it difficult to navigate. I stopped and looked around a few times, wondering about the whole concept of the paranormal.

Despite my experience with the first meet-up group, I was a firm believer in ghosts. I'd had a few experiences in my life that I couldn't explain. In some ways, I hoped that by getting closer to the subject, I might gain more insight to the things that had happened to me.

I had a lot of questions.

Seven other people attended, all having various levels of experience. Some of them brought their own equipment, and others, like us, came with nothing more than flashlights and digital recorders. We didn't find anything overly exciting. No one shouted for us to "GET OUT" while we were there, and our meters only flickered a few times. Still though, it was the most fun I'd had in years. I was hooked.

As we were leaving, we mentioned to Sandy that we were going to Waverly Hills Sanatorium in Louisville, Kentucky, the next month. My sister, knowing how much I loved the paranormal, had booked a ghost hunt for my annual pilgrimage back home to Indiana. Sandy was excited to learn this.

"Do you mind if I come with you?" she asked.

I was elated. A real-life ghost hunter was coming with us! I couldn't wait to get home and call my sister, Leah. Instead of wandering around an abandoned Tuberculosis Hospital with no idea what we were doing, we were going with an experienced paranormal investigator.

It would be the beginning of a friendship that would prove very beneficial for both of us.

To continue reading this paranormal true story, this book is available where you purchased *Ghostly Defenses*. It is also available in eBook format.

Made in the USA
Middletown, DE
18 August 2021